Crock&Pot®

The Original and #1 Brand Slow Cooker

Slow Cooker Recipes
for All Occasions

Publications International, Ltd.

Recipe text on pages 6, 14, 18, 22, 24, 26, 28, 32, 36, 40, 42, 48, 50, 51, 56, 58, 64, 76, and 80 © 2007 Sunbeam Products, Inc. doing business as Jarden Consumer Solutions. All other recipe text © Publications International, Ltd.

Crock-Pot® and the Crock-Pot® logo are registered trademarks of Sunbeam Products, Inc. and are used under license by Publications International, Ltd.

Pictured on the front cover: Linguiça & Green Bean Soup *(page 32)*.
Pictured on the back cover (clockwise from top): Chicken Tortilla Soup *(page 80)*, Peach-Pecan Upside-Down Cake *(page 66)*, and Thai Chicken *(page 24)*.

ISBN-13: 978-1-4127-2835-5
ISBN-10: 1-4127-2835-5

Manufactured in China.

8 7 6 5 4 3 2 1

Preparation/Cooking Times: Preparation times are based on the approximate amount of time required to assemble the recipe before cooking, baking, chilling, or serving. These times include preparation steps such as measuring, chopping, and mixing. The fact that some preparations and cooking can be done simultaneously is taken into account. Preparation of optional ingredients and serving suggestions is not included.

Table of Contents

Impress Your Guests

FABULOUS FARE FOR ALL KINDS OF ENTERTAINING OCCASIONS

Maple-Glazed Meatballs

MAKES ABOUT 48 MEATBALLS

PREP TIME: 10 MINUTES

COOK TIME: 5 TO 6 HOURS (LOW)

- 1½ cups ketchup
- 1 cup maple syrup or maple-flavored syrup
- ⅓ cup reduced-sodium soy sauce
- 1 tablespoon quick-cooking tapioca
- 1½ teaspoons ground allspice
- 1 teaspoon dry mustard
- 2 packages (about 16 ounces each) frozen fully cooked meatballs, partially thawed and separated
- 1 can (20 ounces) pineapple chunks in juice, drained

1. Combine ketchup, maple syrup, soy sauce, tapioca, allspice and mustard in **CROCK-POT**® slow cooker. Carefully stir meatballs and pineapple chunks into ketchup mixture.

2. Cover; cook on LOW 5 to 6 hours. Stir before serving. Insert cocktail picks to serve.

MAKES 6 TO 8 SERVINGS

PREP TIME: 10 MINUTES

COOK TIME: 3 TO 3½ HOURS (LOW) ■ 2 TO 2½ HOURS (HIGH)

3 to 4 cups diced crusty bread (¾- to 1-inch dice)
½ pound bacon, cut into ½-inch dice
2 cups sliced mushrooms
2 cups torn fresh spinach
8 eggs
½ cup milk
¾ cup roasted red peppers, drained and chopped
1 cup shredded cheese, such as Cheddar or Monterey Jack
Salt and black pepper, to taste

1. Coat **CROCK-POT**® slow cooker with nonstick cooking spray. Add bread.

2. Heat skillet on medium heat until hot. Cook bacon until crispy. Remove and discard all but 1 tablespoon of drippings. Add mushrooms and spinach to skillet and toss to coat. Cook 1 to 2 minutes or until spinach wilts.

3. Beat eggs and milk in medium bowl. Stir in red peppers, cheese, salt and black pepper. Pour into **CROCK-POT**® slow cooker.

4. Cover; cook on LOW 3 to 3½ hours or on HIGH 2 to 2½ hours, until eggs are firm but still moist. Adjust seasonings, if desired.

Chocolate Chip Lemon Loaf

MAKES 8 SERVINGS

PREP TIME: 20 TO 30 MINUTES

COOK TIME: 3 TO 4 HOURS (LOW) ■ 1¾ TO 2 HOURS (HIGH)

¾ **cup sugar**

½ **cup shortening**

2 **eggs, lightly beaten**

1⅔ **cups all-purpose flour**

1½ **teaspoons baking powder**

¼ **teaspoon salt**

¾ **cup milk**

½ **cup chocolate chips**

Grated peel of 1 lemon

Juice of 1 lemon

¼ **to ½ cup powdered sugar**

Melted chocolate (optional)

1. Coat **CROCK-POT**® slow cooker with butter or nonstick cooking spray. Beat sugar and shortening in large bowl until blended. Add eggs, one at a time, mixing well after each addition.

2. Sift together flour, baking powder and salt. Add flour mixture and milk alternately to shortening mixture. Stir in chocolate chips and lemon peel.

3. Spoon batter into **CROCK-POT**® slow cooker. Cook, covered, with lid slightly ajar to allow excess moisture to escape, on LOW 3 to 4 hours or on HIGH 1¾ to 2 hours or until edges are golden and knife inserted into center of loaf comes out clean. Remove stoneware from **CROCK-POT**® base. Cool on wire rack about 10 minutes; remove loaf from stoneware and cool completely on rack.

4. Combine lemon juice and ¼ cup powdered sugar in small bowl until smooth. Add more sugar, as needed, to reach desired glaze consistency. Pour glaze over loaf. Drizzle loaf with melted chocolate, if desired.

Deluxe Potato Casserole

MAKES 8 TO 10 SERVINGS

PREP TIME: 10 MINUTES

COOK TIME: 8 TO 10 HOURS (LOW) ■ 5 TO 6 HOURS (HIGH)

- 1 can (10¾ ounces) condensed cream of chicken soup
- 1 container (8 ounces) sour cream
- ¼ cup chopped onion
- ¼ cup plus 3 tablespoons melted butter, divided
- 1 teaspoon salt
- 2 pounds potatoes, peeled and chopped
- 2 cups (8 ounces) shredded Cheddar cheese
- 1½ to 2 cups stuffing mix

1. Combine soup, sour cream, onion, ¼ cup butter and salt in small bowl.

2. Combine potatoes and cheese in **CROCK-POT**® slow cooker. Pour soup mixture over potato mixture; mix well. Sprinkle stuffing mix over potato mixture; drizzle with remaining 3 tablespoons butter.

3. Cover; cook on LOW 8 to 10 hours or on HIGH 5 to 6 hours or until potatoes are tender.

Chai Tea

MAKES 8 TO 10 SERVINGS

PREP TIME: 8 MINUTES

COOK TIME: 2 TO 2½ HOURS (HIGH)

  2 quarts (8 cups) water
  8 bags black tea
  ¾ cup sugar*
 16 whole cloves
 16 whole cardamom seeds, pods removed (optional)
  5 cinnamon sticks
  8 slices fresh ginger
  1 cup milk

Chai tea is typically a sweet drink. For less sweetness, reduce sugar to ½ cup.

1. Combine water, tea, sugar, cloves, cardamom, if desired, cinnamon and ginger in **CROCK-POT**® slow cooker. Cover; cook on HIGH 2 to 2½ hours.

2. Strain mixture; discard solids. (At this point, tea may be covered and refrigerated for up to 3 days.)

3. Stir in milk just before serving. Serve warm or chilled.

Cran-Cherry Bread Pudding

MAKES 12 SERVINGS

PREP TIME: 20 TO 25 MINUTES

COOK TIME: 3½ TO 5½ HOURS (LOW)

    3 **large egg yolks, beaten**
1½ **cups light cream**
 ⅓ **cup sugar**
 ¼ **teaspoon kosher salt**
1½ **teaspoons cherry extract**
 ⅔ **cup sweetened dried cranberries**
 ⅔ **cup golden raisins**
 ½ **cup whole candied red cherries, cut in half**
 ¾ **cup sherry**
    9 **cups unseasoned bread stuffing croutons or 18 slices bread, dried in oven and cut into ½-inch cubes**
    1 **cup white chocolate baking chips**
       Whipped cream

1. Coat **CROCK-POT**® slow cooker with butter or nonstick cooking spray. Combine egg yolks, cream, sugar and salt in medium heavy saucepan. Cook and stir over medium heat until mixture thickens enough to coat metal spoon. Remove custard from heat; cool at once by setting saucepan in sink of ice water and stirring 1 to 2 minutes. Stir in cherry extract. Place custard in a large mixing bowl. Cover surface with clear plastic wrap; refrigerate.

2. Combine cranberries, raisins and cherries in small bowl. Heat sherry until warm. Pour over fruits; set aside 10 minutes.

3. Fold bread cubes and baking chips into custard, until coated. Drain fruits, reserving sherry. Mix fruits with bread cube mixture. Pour bread and fruit mixture into **CROCK-POT**® slow cooker. Lightly press with back of spoon. Pour reserved sherry over bread mixture.

4. Cover; cook on LOW 3½ to 5½ hours or until pudding springs back when touched. Remove stoneware from **CROCK-POT**® base. Cool on wire rack about 10 minutes. Serve warm with whipped cream.

Cran-Orange Acorn Squash

MAKES 6 SERVINGS

PREP TIME: 20 MINUTES

COOK TIME: 2½ HOURS (LOW)

3 small acorn or carnival squash
5 tablespoons instant brown rice
3 tablespoons minced onion
3 tablespoons diced celery
3 tablespoons dried cranberries
 Pinch ground or dried sage leaves
1 teaspoon butter, cut into small pieces
3 tablespoons orange juice
½ cup water

1. Slice off tops of squash and enough of bottoms so squash will sit upright. Scoop out seeds and discard; set squash aside.

2. Combine rice, onion, celery, cranberries and sage in small bowl. Stuff each squash with rice mixture; dot with butter. Pour 1 tablespoon orange juice into each squash over stuffing. Stand squash in **CROCK-POT**® slow cooker. Pour water into bottom.

3. Cover; cook on LOW 2½ hours or until squash are tender.

Tip: To make slicing off tops and bottoms easier, microwave whole squash on HIGH 5 minutes.

Scalloped Tomatoes and Corn

MAKES 4 TO 6 SERVINGS

PREP TIME: 7 MINUTES

COOK TIME: 4 TO 6 HOURS (LOW)

- **1 can (15 ounces) cream-style corn**
- **1 can (14½ ounces) diced tomatoes, undrained**
- **¾ cup saltine cracker crumbs**
- **1 egg, lightly beaten**
- **2 teaspoons sugar**
- **¾ teaspoon black pepper**

Combine corn, tomatoes with juice, cracker crumbs, egg, sugar and pepper in **CROCK-POT**® slow cooker; mix well. Cover; cook on LOW 4 to 6 hours or until done.

Spicy Sweet & Sour Mini-Franks

MAKES ABOUT 4 DOZEN

PREP TIME: 8 MINUTES

COOK TIME: 2 TO 3 HOURS (LOW)

- **2 packages (8 ounces each) mini-franks**
- **½ cup ketchup or chili sauce**
- **½ cup apricot preserves**
- **1 teaspoon hot pepper sauce, plus additional, if desired**

Combine mini-franks, ketchup, preserves and hot sauce in **CROCK-POT**® slow cooker; mix well. Cover; cook on LOW 2 to 3 hours. Serve warm or at room temperature with additional hot sauce, if desired.

Stuffed Chicken Breasts

MAKES 6 SERVINGS

PREP TIME: 20 MINUTES

COOK TIME: 5½ TO 6 HOURS (LOW) ■ 4 HOURS (HIGH)

- 6 boneless skinless chicken breasts
- 8 ounces feta cheese, crumbled
- 3 cups chopped fresh spinach leaves
- ⅓ cup oil-packed sun-dried tomatoes, drained and chopped
- 1 teaspoon minced lemon peel
- 1 teaspoon dried basil, oregano or mint
- ½ teaspoon garlic powder
  Freshly ground black pepper, to taste
- 1 can (15 ounces) diced tomatoes, undrained
- ½ cup oil-cured olives*
  Hot cooked polenta

If using pitted olives, add to CROCK-POT® slow cooker in final hour of cooking.

1. Place chicken breast between 2 pieces of plastic wrap. Using tenderizer mallet or back of skillet, pound breast until about ¼ inch thick. Repeat with remaining chicken.

2. Combine feta, spinach, sun-dried tomatoes, lemon peel, basil, garlic powder and pepper in medium bowl.

3. Lay pounded chicken, smooth side down, on work surface. Place approximately 2 tablespoons feta mixture on wide end of breast. Roll tightly. Repeat with remaining chicken.

4. Place rolled chicken, seam side down, in **CROCK-POT**® slow cooker. Top with diced tomatoes with juice and olives.

5. Cover; cook on LOW 5½ to 6 hours or on HIGH 4 hours. Serve with polenta.

Pizza Fondue

MAKES 20 TO 25 APPETIZER SERVINGS

PREP TIME: 15 MINUTES

COOK TIME: 3 TO 4 HOURS (LOW)

½ pound bulk Italian sausage

1 cup chopped onion

2 jars (26 ounces each) meatless pasta sauce

4 ounces thinly sliced ham, finely chopped

1 package (3 ounces) sliced pepperoni, finely chopped

¼ teaspoon crushed red pepper flakes

1 pound mozzarella cheese, cut into ¾-inch cubes

1 loaf Italian or French bread, cut into 1-inch cubes

1. Cook and stir sausage and onion in large skillet over medium-high heat until sausage is browned. Drain and discard fat. Transfer sausage to **CROCK-POT**® slow cooker. Stir in pasta sauce, ham, pepperoni and pepper flakes. Cover; cook on LOW 3 to 4 hours.

2. Serve warm fondue with cheese and bread cubes.

MAKES ABOUT 6 CUPS

PREP TIME: 10 TO 15 MINUTES

COOK TIME: 30 MINUTES TO 1 HOUR (HIGH) PLUS 2 TO 4 HOURS (LOW)

- ½ cup butter
- 6 stalks celery, sliced
- 2 onions, chopped
- 2 cans (4 ounces each) sliced mushrooms, drained
- ¼ cup plus 2 tablespoons flour
- 2 cans (10¾ ounces each) condensed cream of celery soup
- 5 to 6 ounces garlic cheese, cut into cubes
- 2 packages (10 ounces each) frozen broccoli spears
  French bread slices, bell pepper strips, cherry tomatoes

1. Melt butter in large skillet. Add celery, onion and mushrooms; cook and stir until translucent. Stir in flour and cook 2 to 3 minutes. Transfer to **CROCK-POT**® slow cooker.

2. Stir in soup, cheese and broccoli. Cover; cook on HIGH, stirring every 15 minutes, until cheese is melted. Turn **CROCK-POT**® slow cooker to LOW. Cover; cook 2 to 4 hours or until ready to serve.

3. Serve warm with bread slices or assorted vegetables, as desired.

World-Class Cuisine

FESTIVE RECIPES FROM THE MOST POPULAR CUISINES AROUND THE WORLD

Thai Chicken

MAKES 6 SERVINGS

PREP TIME: 10 TO 15 MINUTES

COOK TIME: 8 TO 9 HOURS (LOW) ■ 3 TO 4 HOURS (HIGH)

2½ pounds chicken pieces
1 cup hot salsa
¼ cup peanut butter
2 tablespoons lime juice
1 tablespoon soy sauce
1 teaspoon minced fresh ginger
Hot cooked rice
½ cup peanuts, chopped
2 tablespoons chopped fresh cilantro

1. Place chicken in **CROCK-POT**® slow cooker. Combine salsa, peanut butter, lime juice, soy sauce and ginger; pour over chicken.

2. Cover; cook on LOW 8 to 9 hours or on HIGH 3 to 4 hours, or until done.

3. Serve chicken and sauce over rice; sprinkle with peanuts and cilantro.

Cioppino

MAKES 6 SERVINGS

1 pound cod, halibut, or any firm-fleshed white fish, cubed
1 cup mushrooms, sliced
2 carrots, sliced
1 onion, chopped
1 green bell pepper, chopped
1 teaspoon minced garlic
1 can (15 ounces) tomato sauce
1 can (14 ounces) beef broth
1 teaspoon salt
½ teaspoon black pepper
½ teaspoon dried oregano
1 can (7 ounces) cooked clams
½ pound cooked shrimp
1 package (6 ounces) cooked crabmeat
Minced parsley

1. Combine fish pieces, mushrooms, carrots, onion, bell pepper, garlic, tomato sauce, broth, salt, black pepper and oregano in **CROCK-POT**® slow cooker. Cover; cook on LOW 10 to 12 hours.

2. Turn **CROCK-POT**® slow cooker to HIGH. Add clams, shrimp and crabmeat. Cover; cook 15 to 30 minutes or until seafood is heated through. Garnish with parsley before serving.

Mediterranean Chicken

MAKES 6 SERVINGS

PREP TIME: 15 TO 20 MINUTES

COOK TIME: 8 TO 10 HOURS (LOW) ■ 4 TO 5 HOURS (HIGH)

- 1 tablespoon olive oil
- 2 pounds boneless skinless chicken breasts
- 1 can (28 ounces) diced tomatoes, undrained
- 2 onions, chopped
- ½ cup sherry
  Juice of 2 lemons
- 6 teaspoons minced garlic
- 2 cinnamon sticks
- 1 bay leaf
- ½ teaspoon black pepper
- 1 pound cooked broad noodles
- ½ cup feta cheese

1. Heat oil in large skillet over medium heat until hot. Add chicken and cook to brown both sides, 2 to 3 minutes per side; set aside.

2. Combine tomatoes with juice, onions, sherry, lemon juice, garlic, cinnamon, bay leaf and pepper in **CROCK-POT**® slow cooker. Add chicken. Cover; cook on LOW 8 to 10 hours or on HIGH 4 to 5 hours, or until done.

3. Remove cinnamon sticks and bay leaf. Serve chicken and sauce over cooked noodles. Sprinkle with cheese just before serving.

Caribbean Sweet Potato & Bean Stew

MAKES 4 SERVINGS

2 medium sweet potatoes (about 1 pound), peeled and cut into 1-inch cubes

2 cups frozen cut green beans

1 can (15 ounces) black beans, rinsed and drained

1 can (14½ ounces) vegetable broth

1 small onion, sliced

2 teaspoons Caribbean jerk seasoning

½ teaspoon dried thyme

¼ teaspoon salt

¼ teaspoon ground cinnamon

Salt and black pepper, to taste

⅓ cup slivered almonds, toasted*

Hot pepper sauce (optional)

To toast almonds, spread in single layer in heavy-bottomed skillet. Cook over medium heat 1 to 2 minutes, stirring frequently, until nuts are lightly browned. Remove from skillet immediately. Cool before using.

1. Combine sweet potatoes, beans, broth, onion, jerk seasoning, thyme, salt and cinnamon in **CROCK-POT**® slow cooker.

2. Cover; cook on LOW 5 to 6 hours or until vegetables are tender.

3. Adjust seasonings. Sprinkle with almonds. Serve with hot sauce, if desired.

Linguiça & Green Bean Soup

MAKES 6 SERVINGS

PREP TIME: 20 MINUTES

COOK TIME: 8 TO 10 HOURS (LOW) ■ 4 TO 6 HOURS (HIGH)

- 1 large yellow onion, chopped
- 3 cloves garlic, minced
- 2 tablespoons olive oil
- 1 cup tomato juice
- 4 cups of water
- 1 tablespoon Italian seasoning
- 2 teaspoons garlic salt
- 1 teaspoon ground cumin
- 1 bay leaf
- 2 cans (16 ounces each) cut green beans, drained
- 1 can (16 ounces) kidney beans, drained
- 1 pound fried linguiça sausage, cut into bite-sized pieces

1. Add all ingredients to **CROCK-POT**® slow cooker. Cover and cook on LOW 8 to 10 hours or on HIGH 4 to 6 hours. Add more boiling water during cooking, if necessary.

2. Serve with warm cornbread.

Risi Bisi

MAKES 6 SERVINGS

- 1½ cups converted long-grain white rice
- ¾ cup chopped onion
- 2 cloves garlic, minced
- 2 cans (14½ ounces each) reduced-sodium chicken broth
- ⅓ cup water
- ¾ teaspoon Italian seasoning
- ½ teaspoon dried basil
- ½ cup frozen peas, thawed
- ¼ cup grated Parmesan cheese
- ¼ cup toasted pine nuts (optional)

1. Combine rice, onion and garlic in **CROCK-POT**® slow cooker. Bring broth and water to a boil in small saucepan. Stir boiling liquid, Italian seasoning and basil into rice mixture. Cover; cook on LOW 2 to 3 hours or until liquid is absorbed.

2. Add peas. Cover; cook 1 hour. Stir in cheese. Spoon rice into serving bowl. Sprinkle with pine nuts, if desired.

Ratatouille with Garbanzo Beans

MAKES 6 TO 8 SERVINGS

PREP TIME: 15 MINUTES

COOK TIME: 7 TO 8 HOURS (LOW) ■ 4½ TO 5 HOURS (HIGH)

  3 tablespoons olive oil, divided
  4 cloves garlic, minced
  1 yellow onion, cut into ½-inch dice
  4 small Italian eggplants, peeled and cut into ¾- to 1-inch dice
     Salt and black pepper, to taste
  1 red bell pepper, seeded and cut into ¾- to 1-inch dice
  1 yellow bell pepper, seeded and cut into ¾- to 1-inch dice
  1 orange bell pepper, seeded and cut into ¾- to 1-inch dice
  3 small zucchini, cut into ¾-inch dice
  1 can (15 to 20 ounces) garbanzo beans, rinsed and drained
  2 cups crushed tomatoes
  ¼ cup fresh basil
  2 tablespoons chopped fresh thyme
  ½ to 1 teaspoon crushed red pepper flakes
     Fresh basil for garnish (optional)

1. Heat 1 tablespoon oil in skillet on medium-low until hot. Add garlic and onion, and cook 2 to 3 minutes or until translucent. Add eggplants, season with salt and black pepper, and cook 1 to 2 minutes. Turn heat to low and cover. Cook 4 to 5 minutes, or until eggplants are tender. Transfer to **CROCK-POT**® slow cooker.

2. Add bell peppers, zucchini and garbanzo beans.

3. Combine tomatoes, basil, thyme, pepper flakes and remaining 2 tablespoons oil in medium bowl; stir well. Pour into **CROCK-POT**® slow cooker. Stir together all ingredients.

4. Cover; cook on LOW 7 to 8 hours or on HIGH 4½ to 5 hours, or until vegetables are tender. Adjust seasonings. Garnish with basil, if desired.

Spectacular Sides

APPEALING ACCOMPANIMENTS FOR MEALTIME VARIETY

Asparagus and Cheese

MAKES 4 TO 6 SERVINGS

PREP TIME: 10 MINUTES

COOK TIME: 3 TO 3½ HOURS (HIGH)

- 2 cups crushed saltine crackers
- 1 can (10¾ ounces) condensed cream of asparagus soup
- 1 can (10¾ ounces) condensed cream of chicken soup
- ⅔ cup slivered almonds
- 4 ounces American cheese, cut into cubes
- 1 egg
- 1½ pounds fresh asparagus, trimmed

Combine crackers, soups, almonds, cheese and egg in large bowl; stir well. Pour into **CROCK-POT**® slow cooker. Add asparagus and stir to coat. Cover; cook on HIGH 3 to 3½ hours or until asparagus is tender.

Wild Rice and Mushroom Casserole

MAKES 4 TO 6 SERVINGS

PREP TIME: 10 TO 15 MINUTES

COOK TIME: 4 TO 6 HOURS (LOW) ■ 2 TO 3 HOURS (HIGH)

- 2 tablespoons olive oil
- ½ medium red onion, finely diced
- 1 large green bell pepper, finely diced
- 8 ounces button mushrooms, thinly sliced
- 2 cloves garlic, minced
- 1 can (14 ounces) diced tomatoes, drained
- 1 teaspoon dried oregano
- 1 teaspoon paprika
- 2 tablespoons butter
- 2 tablespoons all-purpose flour
- 1½ cups milk
- 8 ounces pepper-jack, Cheddar or Swiss cheese, shredded
- 1 teaspoon salt
- ½ teaspoon black pepper
- 2 cups wild rice, cooked according to package instructions

1. Coat **CROCK-POT**® slow cooker with nonstick cooking spray.

2. Heat oil in large skillet over medium heat until hot. Add onion, bell pepper and mushrooms. Cook and stir 5 to 6 minutes, or until vegetables soften. Add garlic, tomatoes, oregano and paprika. Continue to cook and stir until heated through. Transfer to large mixing bowl to cool.

3. Melt butter in same skillet over medium heat; whisk in flour. Cook and stir until smooth and golden, about 4 to 5 minutes. Whisk in milk and bring to a boil. Whisk shredded cheese into boiling milk, stirring to produce rich, velvety sauce. Stir in salt and black pepper.

4. Combine cooked wild rice with vegetables in large mixing bowl. Fold in cheese sauce and mix gently. Pour into **CROCK-POT**® slow cooker. Cover; cook on LOW 4 to 6 hours or on HIGH 2 to 3 hours or until done.

Supper Squash Medley

MAKES 8 TO 10 SERVINGS

- 2 butternut squash, peeled, seeded and diced
- 1 can (28 ounces) tomatoes, undrained
- 1 can (15 ounces) corn, drained
- 2 onions, chopped
- 2 teaspoons minced garlic
- 2 green chilies, chopped
- 2 green bell peppers, chopped
- 1 cup chicken broth
- 1 teaspoon salt
- ½ teaspoon black pepper
- 1 can (6 ounces) tomato paste

1. Combine squash, tomatoes with juice, corn, onions, garlic, chilies, bell peppers, broth, salt and black pepper in **CROCK-POT**® slow cooker. Cover; cook on LOW 6 hours.

2. Remove about ½ cup cooking liquid and blend with tomato paste. Add back to **CROCK-POT**® slow cooker and stir well. Cook 30 minutes or until slightly thickened and heated through.

Orange-Spiced Sweet Potatoes

MAKES 8 SERVINGS

PREP TIME: 10 TO 15 MINUTES

COOK TIME: 4 HOURS (LOW) ■ 2 HOURS (HIGH)

- 2 pounds sweet potatoes, peeled and diced
- ½ cup packed dark brown sugar
- ½ cup butter (1 stick), cut into small pieces
- 1 teaspoon ground cinnamon
- ½ teaspoon ground nutmeg
- ½ teaspoon grated orange peel
  Juice of 1 medium orange
- ¼ teaspoon salt
- 1 teaspoon vanilla
  Chopped toasted pecans (optional)

Place sweet potatoes, brown sugar, butter, cinnamon, nutmeg, orange peel, orange juice, salt and vanilla in **CROCK-POT**® slow cooker. Cover; cook on LOW 4 hours or on HIGH 2 hours, or until potatoes are tender. Sprinkle with pecans before serving, if desired.

Variation: Mash potatoes; add ¼ cup milk or whipping cream. Sprinkle with a mixture of sugar and cinnamon.

Scalloped Potatoes and Parsnips

MAKES 4 TO 6 SERVINGS

PREP TIME: 15 TO 20 MINUTES

COOK TIME: 7 HOURS (LOW) ■ 3½ HOURS (HIGH)

- 6 tablespoons unsalted butter
- 3 tablespoons all-purpose flour
- 1¾ cups heavy cream
- 2 teaspoons dry mustard
- 1½ teaspoons salt
- 1 teaspoon dried thyme
- ½ teaspoon black pepper
- 2 baking potatoes, peeled, cut in half lengthwise, then cut into ¼-inch slices crosswise
- 2 parsnips, peeled and cut into ¼-inch slices
- 1 onion, chopped
- 2 cups (8 ounces) shredded sharp Cheddar cheese

1. For cream sauce: Melt butter in medium saucepan over medium-high heat. Whisk in flour and cook and stir 1 to 2 minutes. Slowly whisk in cream, mustard, salt, thyme and pepper. Stir until smooth.

2. Place potatoes, parsnips and onion in **CROCK-POT**® slow cooker. Add cream sauce. Cover; cook on LOW 7 hours or on HIGH 3½ hours, or until potatoes are tender.

3. Stir in cheese. Cover; let stand until cheese melts.

Corn on the Cob with Garlic Herb Butter

MAKES 4 TO 5 SERVINGS

PREP TIME: 10 TO 15 MINUTES

COOK TIME: 4 TO 5 HOURS (LOW) ■ 2 TO 2½ HOURS (HIGH)

  1 stick unsalted butter, at room temperature
  3 to 4 cloves garlic, minced
  2 tablespoons finely minced fresh parsley
  4 to 5 ears of corn, husked
     Salt and black pepper, to taste

1. Thoroughly mix butter, garlic and parsley in small bowl.

2. Place each ear of corn on a piece of aluminum foil and generously spread butter on each ear. Season corn with salt and pepper and tightly seal foil. Place corn in **CROCK-POT**® slow cooker; overlap ears, if necessary. Add enough water to come one-fourth of the way up each ear.

3. Cover; cook on LOW 4 to 5 hours or on HIGH 2 to 2½ hours, or until done.

Red Cabbage and Apples

MAKES 4 TO 6 SERVINGS

PREP TIME: 15 TO 20 MINUTES

COOK TIME: 6 HOURS (HIGH)

- **1 small head red cabbage, cored and thinly sliced**
- **3 medium apples, peeled and grated**
- **¼ cup sugar**
- **½ cup red wine vinegar**
- **1 teaspoon ground cloves**
- **1 cup crisp-cooked and crumbled bacon (optional)**
- **Fresh apple slices (optional)**

Combine cabbage, apples, sugar, vinegar and cloves in **CROCK-POT**® slow cooker. Cover; cook on HIGH 6 hours, stirring after 3 hours. To serve, sprinkle with bacon and garnish with apple slices, if desired.

Vegetable Curry

MAKES 6 SERVINGS

PREP TIME: 10 TO 15 MINUTES

COOK TIME: 8 TO 9 HOURS (LOW)

- **4 potatoes, diced**
- **1 onion, chopped**
- **1 red bell pepper, chopped**
- **2 carrots, diced**
- **2 tomatoes, chopped**
- **1 can (6 ounces) tomato paste**
- **¾ cup water**
- **2 teaspoons cumin seeds**
- **½ teaspoon garlic powder**
- **½ teaspoon salt**
- **3 cups cauliflower**
- **1 package (10 ounces) frozen peas, thawed**

Combine potatoes, onion, bell pepper, carrots and tomatoes in **CROCK-POT**® slow cooker. Stir in tomato paste, water, cumin seeds, garlic powder and salt. Add cauliflower; stir well. Cover; cook on LOW 8 to 9 hours, or until vegetables are tender. Stir in peas before serving.

Pesto Rice and Beans

MAKES 8 SERVINGS

PREP TIME: 5 MINUTES

COOK TIME: 3 HOURS (LOW)

- 1 can (15 ounces) great Northern beans, rinsed and drained
- 1 can (14 ounces) chicken broth
- ¾ cup uncooked converted long-grain rice
- 1½ cups frozen cut green beans, thawed and drained
- ½ cup prepared pesto
  Grated Parmesan cheese (optional)

1. Combine beans, broth and rice in **CROCK-POT**® slow cooker. Cover; cook on LOW 2 hours.

2. Stir in green beans. Cover; cook 1 hour or until rice and beans are tender. Turn off **CROCK-POT**® slow cooker and transfer stoneware to heatproof surface. Stir in pesto and Parmesan cheese, if desired. Let stand, covered, 5 minutes or until cheese is melted. Serve immediately.

Creamy Curried Spinach

MAKES 6 TO 8 SERVINGS

PREP TIME: 10 TO 15 MINUTES

COOK TIME: 3 TO 4 HOURS (LOW) ■ 2 HOURS (HIGH)

- 3 packages (10 ounces each) frozen spinach, thawed
- 1 onion, chopped
- 4 teaspoons minced garlic
- 2 tablespoons curry powder
- 2 tablespoons butter, melted
- ¼ cup chicken broth
- ¼ cup heavy cream
- 1 teaspoon lemon juice

Combine spinach, onion, garlic, curry powder, butter, and broth in **CROCK-POT**® slow cooker. Cover; cook on LOW 3 to 4 hours or on HIGH 2 hours, or until done. Stir in cream and lemon juice 30 minutes before end of cooking time.

Sweet Endings

FRESH, TASTY DESSERTS FOR THE PERFECT FINISH

Cherry Flan

MAKES 6 SERVINGS

PREP TIME: 10 MINUTES

COOK TIME: 3½ TO 4 HOURS (LOW)

5 eggs
½ cup sugar
½ teaspoon salt
¾ cup all-purpose flour
1 can (12 ounces) evaporated milk
1 teaspoon vanilla
1 bag (16 ounces) frozen pitted, dark sweet cherries, thawed
Whipped cream or cherry vanilla ice cream

1. Coat **CROCK-POT**® slow cooker with butter or nonstick cooking spray.

2. Beat eggs, sugar and salt in large bowl with electric mixer at high speed until thick and pale yellow. Add flour; beat until smooth. Beat in evaporated milk and vanilla.

3. Pour batter into **CROCK-POT**® slow cooker. Place cherries evenly over batter. Cover; cook on LOW 3½ to 4 hours or until flan is set. Serve warm with whipped cream.

Decadent Chocolate Delight

MAKES 12 SERVINGS

PREP TIME: 5 TO 10 MINUTES

COOK TIME: 3 TO 4 HOURS (LOW) ■ 1½ TO 1¾ HOURS (HIGH)

1 package (about 18 ounces) chocolate cake mix

1 container (8 ounces) sour cream

1 cup semisweet chocolate chips

1 cup water

4 eggs

¾ cup vegetable oil

1 package (4-serving size) instant chocolate pudding and pie filling mix

1. Coat **CROCK-POT**® slow cooker with butter or nonstick cooking spray.

2. Combine all ingredients in medium bowl; mix well. Transfer to **CROCK-POT**® slow cooker.

3. Cover; cook on LOW 6 to 8 hours or on HIGH 3 to 4 hours. Serve hot or warm with ice cream.

HELPFUL HINTS

Keep these general guidelines in mind when making delicious desserts and baked goods in your **CROCK-POT**® slow cooker:

● Do not overbeat cake and bread batters. Follow all recommended mixing times.

● Do not add water to the **CROCK-POT**® slow cooker unless instructed to do so in the recipe.

● After cakes and breads have finished cooking, allow them to cool in the stoneware at least 5 minutes before removing.

Strawberry Rhubarb Crisp

MAKES 8 SERVINGS

PREP TIME: 20 MINUTES

COOK TIME: 1½ HOURS (HIGH) PLUS 15 TO 20 MINUTES (375°F OVEN)

Fruit filling

- 4 cups sliced hulled strawberries
- 4 cups diced rhubarb (about 5 stalks), cut into ½-inch dice
- 1½ cups granulated sugar
- 2 tablespoons lemon juice
- 1½ tablespoons cornstarch, plus water (optional)

Topping

- 1 cup all-purpose flour
- 1 cup old-fashioned oats
- ½ cup granulated sugar
- ½ cup packed brown sugar
- ½ teaspoon ground ginger
- ½ teaspoon ground nutmeg
- ½ cup (1 stick) butter, cut into small pieces
- ½ cup sliced almonds, toasted*

To toast almonds, spread in single layer in heavy-bottomed skillet. Cook over medium heat 1 to 2 minutes, stirring frequently, until nuts are lightly browned. Remove from skillet immediately. Cool before using.

1. For fruit filling: Coat **CROCK-POT**® slow cooker with butter or nonstick cooking spray. Place strawberries, rhubarb, sugar and lemon juice in **CROCK-POT**® slow cooker; mix well. Cover; cook on HIGH 1½ hours or until fruit is tender.

2. If fruit is dry, add a little water. If fruit has too much liquid, mix cornstarch with a small amount of water and stir into fruit. Cook on HIGH 15 minutes longer, or until cooking liquid has thickened.

3. For topping: Preheat oven to 375°F. Combine flour, oats, sugars, ginger and nutmeg in medium bowl. Cut in butter using pastry blender or 2 knives until mixture resembles small peas. Stir in almonds.

4. Remove lid from **CROCK-POT**® slow cooker; gently sprinkle topping on fruit. Transfer stoneware to oven. Bake 15 to 20 minutes or until topping begins to brown.

"Peachy Keen" Dessert Treat

MAKES 8 TO 12 SERVINGS

PREP TIME: 10 TO 15 MINUTES

COOK TIME: 4 TO 6 HOURS (LOW)

- 1⅓ cups uncooked old-fashioned oats
- 1 cup granulated sugar
- 1 cup packed light brown sugar
- ⅔ cup buttermilk baking mix
- 2 teaspoons ground cinnamon
- ½ teaspoon ground nutmeg
- 2 pounds fresh peaches (about 8 medium), sliced

Coat **CROCK-POT**® slow cooker with nonstick cooking spray. Combine oats, sugars, baking mix, cinnamon and nutmeg in large bowl. Stir in peaches until well blended. Transfer to **CROCK-POT**® slow cooker. Cover; cook on LOW 4 to 6 hours, or until done.

Streusel Pound Cake

MAKES 6 TO 8 SERVINGS

PREP TIME: 10 TO 15 MINUTES

COOK TIME: 1½ TO 1¾ HOURS (HIGH)

- 1 package (16 ounces) pound cake mix, plus ingredients to prepare mix
- ¼ cup packed light brown sugar
- 1 tablespoon all-purpose flour
- ¼ cup chopped nuts
- 1 teaspoon ground cinnamon

Coat **CROCK-POT**® slow cooker with nonstick cooking spray. Prepare cake mix according to package directions; stir in brown sugar, flour, nuts and cinnamon. Pour batter into **CROCK-POT**® slow cooker. Cover; cook on HIGH 1½ to 1¾ hours, or until toothpick inserted into center of cake comes out clean.

"PEACHY KEEN DESSERT TREAT"

Coconut Rice Pudding

MAKES 6 (¾-CUP) SERVINGS

PREP TIME: 30 TO 35 MINUTES

COOK TIME: 4 HOURS (LOW) ■ 2 HOURS (HIGH)

2 cups water
1 cup uncooked converted long-grain rice
1 tablespoon unsalted butter
Pinch salt
2¼ cups evaporated milk
1 can (14 ounces) cream of coconut
½ cup golden raisins
3 egg yolks, beaten
Grated peel of 2 limes
1 teaspoon vanilla
Toasted shredded coconut (optional)

1. Place water, rice, butter and salt in medium saucepan. Bring to rolling boil over high heat, stirring frequently. Reduce heat to low. Cover; cook 10 to 12 minutes. Remove from heat. Let stand, covered, 5 minutes.

2. Coat **CROCK-POT**® slow cooker with nonstick cooking spray. Add evaporated milk, cream of coconut, raisins, egg yolks, lime peel and vanilla; mix well. Add rice; stir until blended.

3. Cover; cook on LOW 4 hours or on HIGH 2 hours. Stir every 30 minutes, if possible. Pudding will thicken as it cools. Top with toasted coconut, if desired.

Baked Ginger Apples

MAKES 4 SERVINGS

- 4 large Red Delicious apples
- ½ cup (1 stick) unsalted butter, melted
- ⅓ cup chopped macadamia nuts
- ¼ cup chopped dried apricots
- 2 tablespoons finely chopped crystallized ginger
- 1 tablespoon packed dark brown sugar
- ¾ cup brandy
- ½ cup vanilla pudding and pie filling mix
- 2 cups heavy cream

1. Slice tops off apples; remove cores. Combine butter, nuts, apricots, ginger and brown sugar in medium bowl. Fill apples with nut mixture. Transfer to **CROCK-POT**® slow cooker. Pour brandy over apples. Cover; cook on LOW 4 hours or on HIGH 2 hours.

2. Gently remove apples from **CROCK-POT**® slow cooker with slotted spoon; keep warm. Combine pudding mix and cream in small bowl. Add to cooking liquid in **CROCK-POT**® slow cooker; stir well. Turn heat up to HIGH. Cover; cook on HIGH 30 minutes. Stir until smooth. Return apples to **CROCK-POT**® slow cooker; keep warm until ready to serve with warm cream sauce.

Bananas Foster

MAKES 12 SERVINGS

PREP TIME: 5 TO 10 MINUTES

COOK TIME: 1 TO 2 HOURS (LOW)

- 12 bananas, cut into quarters
- 1 cup flaked coconut
- 1 teaspoon ground cinnamon
- ½ teaspoon salt
- 1 cup dark corn syrup
- ⅔ cup butter, melted
- 2 teaspoons grated lemon peel
- ¼ cup lemon juice
- 2 teaspoons rum
- 12 slices pound cake
- 1 quart vanilla ice cream

Combine bananas and coconut in **CROCK-POT**® slow cooker. Combine cinnamon, salt, corn syrup, butter, lemon zest, lemon juice and rum in medium bowl; pour over bananas. Cover; cook on LOW 1 to 2 hours. To serve, arrange bananas on pound cake slices. Top with ice cream and pour on warm sauce.

Peach-Pecan Upside-Down Cake

MAKES 10 SERVINGS

PREP TIME: 10 MINUTES

COOK TIME: 3 HOURS (HIGH)

1	can (8½ ounces) peach slices
⅓	cup packed light brown sugar
2	tablespoons butter or margarine, melted
¼	cup chopped pecans
1	package (16 ounces) pound cake mix, plus ingredients to prepare mix
½	teaspoon almond extract
	Whipped cream (optional)

1. Generously grease 2-quart casserole or soufflé dish that will fit inside **CROCK-POT**® slow cooker stoneware using butter or nonstick cooking spray; set aside.

2. Drain peach slices, reserving 1 tablespoon juice. Combine reserved peach juice, brown sugar and butter in prepared pan. Arrange peach slices on top of brown sugar mixture. Sprinkle with pecans.

3. Prepare cake mix according to package directions; stir in almond extract. Spread over peach mixture. Cover pan with lid or aluminum foil. Make foil handles (see below). Use foil handles to place pan into **CROCK-POT**® slow cooker. Cover; cook on HIGH 3 hours.

4. Remove pan from **CROCK-POT**® slow cooker using foil handles. Cool pan, uncovered, on wire rack 10 minutes. Run narrow spatula around sides of pan; invert onto serving plate. Serve warm with whipped cream, if desired.

Foil handles: Tear off three 18×2-inch strips of heavy foil or use regular foil folded to double thickness. Crisscross foil strips in spoke design and place pan on center of strips. Pull strips up and over pan.

Everyday Favorites

FAST, FAMILY-PLEASING RECIPES FOR EVERY MEAL

Oriental Chicken Wings

MAKES 32 SERVINGS

PREP TIME: 15 TO 20 MINUTES

COOK TIME: 5 TO 6 HOURS (LOW) ■ 2 TO 3 HOURS (HIGH)

16 chicken wings, split and tips removed
1 cup chopped red onion
1 cup soy sauce
¾ cup packed light brown sugar
¼ cup dry cooking sherry
2 tablespoons chopped fresh ginger
2 cloves garlic, minced
Chopped fresh chives

1. Preheat broiler. Broil chicken wings about 5 minutes per side. Transfer to **CROCK-POT**® slow cooker.

2. Combine onion, soy sauce, brown sugar, sherry, ginger and garlic in large bowl. Add to **CROCK-POT**® slow cooker; stir to blend well.

3. Cover and cook on LOW 5 to 6 hours or on HIGH 2 to 3 hours. Sprinkle with chives before serving.

Super Slow Sloppy Joes

MAKES 8 SERVINGS

PREP TIME: 15 TO 20 MINUTES

COOK TIME: 6 TO 8 HOURS (LOW)

- 3 pounds 90% lean ground beef
- 1 cup chopped onion
- 3 cloves garlic, minced
- 1¼ cups ketchup
- 1 cup chopped red bell pepper
- 5 tablespoons Worcestershire sauce
- ¼ cup packed brown sugar
- 3 tablespoons vinegar
- 3 tablespoons prepared mustard
- 2 teaspoons chili powder
- Hamburger buns

1. Brown ground beef, onion and garlic in large nonstick skillet over medium-high heat in 2 batches, stirring to separate meat. Drain and discard fat.

2. Combine ketchup, bell pepper, Worcestershire sauce, brown sugar, vinegar, mustard and chili powder in **CROCK-POT**® slow cooker. Stir in beef mixture.

3. Cover; cook on LOW 6 to 8 hours or until done. Spoon onto hamburger buns.

Three-Bean Turkey Chili

MAKES 6 TO 8 SERVINGS

PREP TIME: 10 TO 15 MINUTES

COOK TIME: 6 TO 8 HOURS (HIGH)

1 pound ground turkey
1 small onion, chopped
1 can (28 ounces) diced tomatoes, undrained
1 can (15 ounces) chickpeas, rinsed and drained
1 can (15 ounces) kidney beans, rinsed and drained
1 can (15 ounces) black beans, rinsed and drained
1 can (8 ounces) tomato sauce
1 can (4 ounces) chopped mild green chilies
1 to 2 tablespoons chili powder

1. Cook and stir turkey and onion in medium skillet over medium-high heat until turkey is no longer pink. Drain and discard fat. Transfer to **CROCK-POT**® slow cooker.

2. Add tomatoes with juice, beans, tomato sauce, chilies and chili powder; mix well. Cover; cook on HIGH 6 to 8 hours or until done.

Orange Date-Nut Bread

MAKES 8 TO 10 SERVINGS

PREP TIME: 10 TO 15 MINUTES

COOK TIME: 1¼ TO 1½ HOURS (HIGH)

 2 cups all-purpose unbleached flour
 1 teaspoon baking powder
 ½ teaspoon baking soda
 ¼ teaspoon salt
 ½ cup chopped pecans
 1 cup chopped dates
 2 teaspoons dried orange peel
 ⅔ cup boiling water
 ¾ cup sugar
 2 tablespoons shortening
 1 egg, lightly beaten
 1 teaspoon vanilla

1. Coat **CROCK-POT**® slow cooker with nonstick cooking spray; set aside. Combine flour, baking powder, baking soda and salt in medium bowl. Mix in pecans; set aside.

2. Combine dates and orange peel in separate medium bowl; pour boiling water over fruit mixture and stir well. Add sugar, shortening, egg and vanilla; stir just until blended. Add flour mixture to date mixture; stir just until blended.

3. Pour batter into **CROCK-POT**® slow cooker. Cover; cook on HIGH 1¼ to 1½ hours, or until edges begin to brown and toothpick inserted into center comes out clean.

4. Remove stoneware from **CROCK-POT**® base. Cool on wire rack about 10 minutes; remove bread from stoneware and cool completely on rack.

Variation: Substitute 1 cup dried cranberries for dates.

Classic Spaghetti

MAKES 6 TO 8 SERVINGS

PREP TIME: 20 TO 30 MINUTES

COOK TIME: 6 TO 8 HOURS (LOW) ■ 3 TO 5 HOURS (HIGH)

2 tablespoons olive oil

2 onions, chopped

2 green bell peppers, sliced

2 stalks celery, sliced

4 teaspoons minced garlic

3 pounds lean ground beef

2 carrots, diced

1 cup sliced mushrooms

1 can (28 ounces) tomato sauce

1 can (28 ounces) stewed tomatoes, undrained

3 cups water

2 tablespoons minced parsley

1 tablespoon dried oregano

1 tablespoon sugar

2 teaspoons salt

2 teaspoons black pepper

1 pound dry spaghetti

1. Heat oil in large skillet over medium-high heat until hot. Add onion, bell pepper, celery and garlic; cook and stir until tender. Transfer to **CROCK-POT**® slow cooker.

2. In same skillet, brown ground beef. Drain and discard fat. Add beef, carrots, mushrooms, tomato sauce, tomatoes with juice, water, parsley, oregano, sugar, salt and black pepper to **CROCK-POT**® slow cooker. Cover; cook on LOW 6 to 8 hours or on HIGH 3 to 5 hours or until done.

3. Cook spaghetti according to package directions; drain. Serve sauce over cooked spaghetti.

Hot & Juicy Reuben Sandwiches

MAKES 4 SERVINGS

PREP TIME: 25 MINUTES

COOK TIME: 7 TO 9 HOURS (LOW)

- 1 mild-cure corned beef (about 1½ pounds)
- 2 cups sauerkraut, drained
- ½ cup beef broth
- 1 small onion, sliced
- 1 clove garlic, minced
- ¼ teaspoon caraway seeds
- 4 to 6 peppercorns
- 8 slices pumpernickel or rye bread
- 4 slices Swiss cheese
  Mustard

1. Trim and discard excess fat from corned beef. Place beef in **CROCK-POT**® slow cooker. Add sauerkraut, broth, onion, garlic, caraway seeds and peppercorns.

2. Cover; cook on LOW 7 to 9 hours.

3. Remove beef from **CROCK-POT**® slow cooker. Cut across grain into 4 (½-inch-thick) slices. Divide evenly among 4 slices bread. Top each slice with ½ cup drained sauerkraut mixture and 1 slice cheese. Spread mustard on remaining 4 bread slices and place on sandwiches.

Chicken Tortilla Soup

MAKES 4 TO 6 SERVINGS

PREP TIME: 10 MINUTES

COOK TIME: 6 HOURS (LOW) ■ 3 HOURS (HIGH)

4 boneless, skinless chicken thighs
2 cans (15 ounces each) diced tomatoes, undrained
1 can (4 ounces) chopped mild green chilies, drained
½ to 1 cup chicken broth
1 yellow onion, diced
2 cloves garlic, minced
1 teaspoon ground cumin
   Salt and black pepper, to taste
4 corn tortillas, sliced into ¼-inch strips
2 tablespoons chopped fresh cilantro
½ cup shredded Monterey Jack cheese
1 avocado, peeled, diced and tossed with lime juice to prevent browning
   Lime wedges

1. Place chicken in **CROCK-POT**® slow cooker. Combine tomatoes with juice, chilies, ½ cup broth, onion, garlic and cumin in small bowl. Pour mixture over chicken.

2. Cover; cook on LOW 6 hours or on HIGH 3 hours, or until chicken is tender. Remove chicken from **CROCK-POT**® slow cooker. Shred with 2 forks. Return to cooking liquid. Adjust seasonings, adding salt and pepper, and more broth if necessary.

3. Just before serving, add tortillas and cilantro to **CROCK-POT**® slow cooker. Stir to blend. Serve in soup bowls, topping each serving with cheese, avocado and a squeeze of lime juice from wedges.

EASY HANDS-ON RECIPES FOR ASPIRING YOUNG CHEFS

Mom's Tuna Casserole

MAKES 8 SERVINGS

PREP TIME: 10 MINUTES

COOK TIME: 5 TO 8 HOURS (LOW)

- 2 **cans (12 ounces each) tuna, drained and flaked**
- 3 **cups diced celery**
- 3 **cups crushed potato chips, divided**
- 6 **hard-cooked eggs, chopped**
- 1 **can (10¾ ounces) condensed cream of mushroom soup**
- 1 **can (10¾ ounces) condensed cream of celery soup**
- 1 **cup mayonnaise**
- 1 **teaspoon dried tarragon**
- 1 **teaspoon black pepper**

1. Combine tuna, celery, 2½ cups chips, eggs, soups, mayonnaise, tarragon and pepper in **CROCK-POT**® slow cooker; stir well.

2. Cover; cook on LOW 5 to 8 hours or until done.

3. Sprinkle with remaining ½ cup chips before serving.

slow cooker Steak Fajitas

MAKES 4 SERVINGS

- **1** beef flank steak (about 1 pound)
- **1** medium onion, cut into strips
- **½** cup medium salsa, plus additional for garnish
- **2** tablespoons fresh lime juice
- **2** tablespoons chopped fresh cilantro
- **2** cloves garlic, minced
- **1** tablespoon chili powder
- **1** teaspoon ground cumin
- **½** teaspoon salt
- **1** small green bell pepper, cut into strips
- **1** small red bell pepper, cut into strips
- Flour tortillas, warmed

1. Cut flank steak lengthwise in half, then crosswise into thin strips. Combine onion, ½ cup salsa, lime juice, cilantro, garlic, chili powder, cumin and salt in **CROCK-POT**® slow cooker. Add steak and stir well. Cover; cook on LOW 5 to 6 hours.

2. Add bell peppers. Cover; cook on LOW 1 hour.

3. Serve with flour tortillas and additional salsa, if desired.

The Best Beef Stew

MAKES 8 SERVINGS

PREP TIME: 20 MINUTES

COOK TIME: 8 TO 12 HOURS (LOW) ■ 4 TO 6 HOURS (HIGH)

- ½ cup plus 2 tablespoons all-purpose flour, divided
- 2 teaspoons salt
- 1 teaspoon black pepper
- 3 pounds beef for stew, cut into 1-inch pieces
- 1 can (16 ounces) diced tomatoes, undrained
- 3 red potatoes, peeled and diced
- ½ pound smoked sausage, sliced
- 1 cup chopped leek
- 1 cup chopped onion
- 4 ribs celery, sliced
- ½ cup chicken broth
- 3 cloves garlic, minced
- 1 teaspoon dried thyme
- 3 tablespoons water

1. Combine ½ cup flour, salt and pepper in resealable plastic food storage bag. Add beef; shake bag to coat beef. Transfer to **CROCK-POT**® slow cooker. Add tomatoes with juice, potatoes, sausage, leek, onion, celery, broth, garlic and thyme; stir well.

2. Cover; cook on LOW 8 to 12 hours or on HIGH 4 to 6 hours. One hour before serving, turn **CROCK-POT**® slow cooker to HIGH. Whisk together remaining 2 tablespoons flour and water in small bowl; stir into **CROCK-POT**® slow cooker. Cover; cook until thickened.

HELPFUL HINTS

You can cook frozen meats in the **CROCK-POT**® slow cooker if you follow these guidelines:

- Do not preheat **CROCK-POT**® slow cooker.
- Add at least 1 cup warm liquid to stoneware before adding meat.
- Cook recipes an additional 4 to 6 hours on LOW or 2 hours on HIGH.

Triple Delicious Hot Chocolate

MAKES 6 SERVINGS

PREP TIME: 10 MINUTES

COOK TIME: 2¼ HOURS (LOW)

- ⅓ cup sugar
- ¼ cup unsweetened cocoa powder
- ¼ teaspoon salt
- 3 cups milk, divided
- ¾ teaspoon vanilla
- 1 cup heavy cream
- 1 square (1 ounce) bittersweet chocolate
- 1 square (1 ounce) white chocolate
- ¾ cup whipped cream
- 6 teaspoons mini chocolate chips or shaved bittersweet chocolate

1. Combine sugar, cocoa, salt and ½ cup milk in medium bowl. Beat until smooth. Pour into **CROCK-POT**® slow cooker. Add remaining 2½ cups milk and vanilla. Cover; cook on LOW 2 hours.

2. Add cream. Cover; cook on LOW 10 to 15 minutes. Stir in bittersweet and white chocolates until melted.

3. Pour hot chocolate into 6 cups. Top each with 2 tablespoons whipped cream and 1 teaspoon chocolate chips.

Southwestern Stuffed Peppers

MAKES 4 SERVINGS

PREP TIME: 15 MINUTES

COOK TIME: 4 TO 6 HOURS (LOW)

- 4 green and/or red bell peppers
- 1 can (15 ounces) black beans, rinsed and drained
- 1 cup (4 ounces) shredded pepper-jack cheese
- ¾ cup medium salsa
- ½ cup frozen whole kernel corn, thawed
- ½ cup chopped green onions with tops
- ⅓ cup uncooked long-grain converted rice
- 1 teaspoon chili powder
- ½ teaspoon ground cumin
- Sour cream (optional)

1. Cut thin slice off top of each bell pepper. Carefully remove seeds, leaving pepper whole.

2. Combine beans, cheese, salsa, corn, onions, rice, chili powder and cumin in medium bowl. Spoon filling evenly into each pepper. Place peppers in **CROCK-POT**® slow cooker.

3. Cover; cook on LOW 4 to 6 hours. Serve with sour cream, if desired.

Mixed Berry Cobbler

MAKES 8 SERVINGS

PREP TIME: 10 MINUTES

COOK TIME: 4 HOURS (LOW)

- **1** package (16 ounces) frozen mixed berries
- **¾** cup granulated sugar
- **2** tablespoons quick-cooking tapioca
- **2** teaspoons grated lemon peel
- **1½** cups all-purpose flour
- **½** cup packed light brown sugar
- **2¼** teaspoons baking powder
- **¼** teaspoon ground nutmeg
- **¾** cup milk
- **⅓** cup butter, melted
  Ice cream (optional)

1. Coat **CROCK-POT**® slow cooker with butter or nonstick cooking spray. Stir together berries, granulated sugar, tapioca and lemon peel in medium bowl. Transfer to **CROCK-POT**® slow cooker.

2. For topping: Combine flour, brown sugar, baking powder and nutmeg in medium bowl. Add milk and butter; stir just until blended. Drop spoonfuls of dough on top of berry mixture.

3. Cover; cook on LOW 4 hours. Uncover; let stand about 30 minutes. Serve with ice cream, if desired.

Three-Cheese Chicken & Noodles

MAKES 6 SERVINGS

PREP TIME: 10 MINUTES

COOK TIME: 6 TO 10 HOURS (LOW) ■ 3 TO 4 HOURS (HIGH)

3 cups chopped cooked chicken

1½ cups cottage cheese

1 can (10¾ ounces) condensed cream of chicken soup

1 package (8 ounces) wide egg noodles, cooked and drained

1 cup diced green and/or red bell pepper

1 cup grated Monterey Jack cheese

½ cup grated Parmesan cheese

½ cup diced celery

½ cup diced onion

½ cup chicken broth

1 can (4 ounces) sliced mushrooms, drained

2 tablespoons butter, melted

½ teaspoon dried thyme

Combine all ingredients in **CROCK-POT**® slow cooker. Stir to coat evenly. Cover; cook on LOW 6 to 10 hours or on HIGH 3 to 4 hours.

Index